ROYAL COURT

Royal Court Theatre presents

THE WOMAN BEFORE

by **Roland Schimmelpfennig**
translated by David Tushingham

First performance at the Royal Court Jerwood Theatre Downstairs, Sloane Square, London on 12 May 2005.

Sponsored by

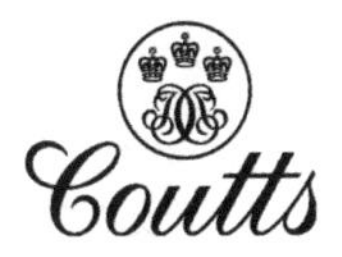

THE WOMAN BEFORE

by **Roland Schimmelpfennig**
translated by David Tushingham

Cast in order of appearance
Frank **Nigel Lindsay**
Claudia **Saskia Reeves**
Romy Vogtländer **Helen Baxendale**
Andi **Robert Pattinson**
Tina **Georgia Taylor**

Director **Richard Wilson**
Designer **Mark Thompson**
Lighting Designer **Johanna Town**
Sound Designer **Ian Dickinson**
Assistant Director **Dan Sherer**
Casting **Lisa Makin**
Production Manager **Paul Handley**
Stage Manager **Maxine Foo**
Deputy Stage Manager **Marius Rønning**
Assistant Stage Manager **Nafeesah Butt**
Costume Supervisor **Iona Kenrick**
Company Voice Work **Patsy Rodenburg**
Fight director **Terry King**

The Royal Court would like to thank the following for their help with this production: A1 House Moving Boxes Ltd, Aylesbury Box Co Ltd, Early Learning Centre, F&N International Removals and Relocation, The Lego Store, Axel Rüger.

THE COMPANY

Roland Schimmelpfennig (writer)
For the Royal Court: Push Up.
Theatre includes: Vorher/Nachher (Frankfurter Positionen); Die Arabische Nacht (Staatstheater Stuttgart/Arabian Night (ATC)); Vor langer Zeit im Mai (Schaubühne, Berlin); MEZ (Schaubühne, Berlin); Keine Arbeit für die junge Frau im Frühlingskleid, Die Zwiefachen (Münchner Kammerspiele); Die ewige Maria (Theater Oberhausen); Fisch um Fisch (Staatstheater Mainz); Aus den Städten in die Wälder, Aus den Wäldern in die Städte (BAT, Berlin); Auf der Greifswalderstraße (Deutsches Theater, Berlin); Ambrosia (Theater Essen); Die Frau von früher (Burgtheater, Wien); Für eine bessere Welt (Schauspiel, Zürich); Alice im Wunderland (Staatstheater Hannover); Angebot und Nachfrage, Push Up (Deutsches Schauspielhaus in Hamburg).
Radio includes: Für eine bessere Welt (Radio play of the year, Hessischer Rundfunk); Angebot und Nachfrage (Hessischer Rundfunk); Die arabische Nacht (Hessischer Rundfunk); Krieg der Wellen (Hessischer Rundfunk, nominee for Radio play of the year), Die Taxiterroristin (Südwestfunk), Vorher/Nachher (Hessischer Rundfunk), Die Aufzeichnung (Südwestfunk).
Translation includes: The Side Man, All the Rage, The Glory of Living, Sling Blade, Penetrator.

Helen Baxendale
Theatre includes: After Miss Julie (Donmar); A Midsummer Night's Dream (Leicester Haymarket); Morning and Evening, Bearing Fruit (Hampstead); Rage (Bush); Soldiers, The Pitchfork Disney, The Marowitz Hamlet, The Hypochondriacs, The Pelican, Summer Lightning (Citizens, Glasgow); East Lynne, Dangerous Corner (Birmingham).
Television includes: The Only Boy For Me, Murder in Mind, Cold Feet, The Capuccino Years, Tales From A Mad House - The Servant Girl, Friends, An Unsuitable Job For a Woman, The Investigator, Crossing the Floor, Truth or Dare, Cardiac Arrest, Marshall and the Madwoman.
Film includes: Skaggerack, Dead by Monday, Ordinary Decent Criminal, Macbeth, Bolshe Vita, Love's Lost Hour.
Awards include: 2000 RTS Best Actress for Servant Girl.

Nigel Lindsay
For the Royal Court: King Lear, Push Up.
Other theatre includes: The Earthly Paradise, The Tower (Almeida); The Pillowman, London Cuckolds, Dealer's Choice (& Vaudeville), Blue Remembered Hills (RNT); World Music, Hamlet (Sheffield Crucible); The Tempest (Old Vic); Bedroom Farce (Aldwych); The Real Thing (Donmar/Albery/Ethel Barrymore Theater, New York); Morphic Resonance (Donmar); Katerina (Lyric, Hammersmith); Relative Values (Salisbury Playhouse); Anna Karenina (Tricycle); Shoot the Archduke (Lilian Bayliss).
Television includes: Life After George, New Tricks, Tunnel of Love, Frances Tuesday, Murphy's Law, My Family, I'm Alan Partridge, Midsomer Murders, The Armando Iannucci Show, Too Much Sun, Déjà vu, A Dance To The Music Of Time, Harbour Lights, Bye Bye Baby, Brass Eye, Dressing For Breakfast, A Few Short Journeys of The Heart, The Bill, Casualty, Between The Lines.
Film includes: On a Clear Day, Blackball, Mike Bassett: England Manager, Rogue Trader.
Radio includes: House of Milton Jones, Frederick & Augusta, Morphic Resonance, People Like Us, Crossing the Equator.

Robert Pattinson
Theatre includes: Our Town, Anything Goes, Tess of the D'Urbervilles (Barnes Theatre Group); Macbeth (OSO Arts Centre).
Film includes: Kingdom in Twilight, Harry Potter & The Goblet of Fire.

Saskia Reeves
For the Royal Court: Ice Cream, King Lear.
Theatre includes: Orpheus Descending (Donmar); The Darker Face of the Earth (RNT); Much Ado About Nothing, Man of Mode, A Midsummer Night's Dream (Cheek By Jowl); Playhouse Creatures (Old Vic); Sweet Panic, Smelling a Rat, Separation (& Comedy) (Hampstead); A Woman Killed By Kindness, 'Tis Pity She's a Whore, Two Gentlemen of Verona, The Virtuoso (RSC); Twelfth Night (Manchester Toyal Exchange); Who's Afraid of Virginia Woolf, Measure for Measure (Young Vic); Metamorphosis (Mermaid).
Televison includes: The Strange Case of Sherlock Holmes, Afterlife, The Commander II, Island at War, Suspicion, Waking the Dead, A Line in the Sand, Dune, Christmas Carol, Plotlands, Perfect Match, Cruel Train, Summer Day's Dream, In My Defence, Antonia and Jane, Children Crossing.
Film includes: The Tesseract, Heart, Faith, Different for Girls, Butterfly Kiss, I.D., The Bridge, Close My Eyes, December Bride.
Awards include: 1987 Plays and Players, London Fringe Award for Best Actress for Who's Afraid of Virgina Woolf, and 1996 Best Actress, Dinard Film Festival for Butterfly Kiss.

Dan Sherer (assistant director)
As assistant director theatre includes: The Fool (Jerwood Vanbrugh Theatre); The America Play (John Gielgud Theatre); Romeo and Juliet (RSC).
As a director theatre includes: The Country, Anna Weiss, Kiss of the Spider Woman, Phaedra's Love, Roberto Zucco (Fringe, Cambridge).
Dan is training as a director at RADA.

Georgia Taylor
Television includes: The Royal, Blackpool, Red Cap, Girls Club, Where the Heart Is, Coronation Street.

Mark Thompson (designer)
For the Royal Court: Six Degrees of Separation (& Comedy); Hysteria (& Mark Taper Forum, Los Angeles); Never Land, The Kitchen, Mouth to Mouth,
Other theatre includes: Insignificance, The Front Page (Donmar); Uncle Vanya, Twelfth Night (costume only, Donmar/BAM); Company (Donmar/Albery); The Blue Room (Donmar/Broadway); Measure for Measure, The Wizard of Oz, Much Ado About Nothing, The Comedy of Errors, Hamlet, The Unexpected Man (RSC); Volpone, Betrayal, Party Time, Butterfly Kiss (Almeida); Henry IV Parts 1 & 2, The Wind in the Willows, The Madness of King George III, Pericles, What the Butler Saw, The Day I Stood Still, The Duchess of Malfi (RNT); Life x 3 (RNT/Old Vic/Broadway); Arcadia (RNT/Haymarket/Lincoln Center, NY), Bombay Dreams (Apollo Victoria/ Broadway); Follies (Broadway); Mamma Mia! (Prince of Wales/ Prince Edward/Broadway/international tours); The Lady in the Van (Queen's); Dr Dolittle (London Apollo/tour); Blast (Apollo/US tour/Broadway); Art (Wyndham's/UK tour, Australia, Buenos Aires, Chicago, Los Angeles & Broadway); Owners (Young Vic); Good (Brussels); The Scarlet Pimpernel (Chichester/Her Majesty's); The Sneeze (Aldwych); Ivanov, Cabaret, Much Ado About Nothing (Strand); A Little Light Music (Piccadilly); Shadowlands (Queen's/Broadway); Joseph and the Amazing Technicolor Dreamcoat (London Palladium/Canadian/Australian/US tours).
Awards include: 1990/91 Olivier Award; Plays and Players and Critics' Award for The Wind in the Willows; 1992 Olivier Awards for Set Design and Costume Design for Joseph And The Amazing Technicolor Dreamcoat and The Comedy Of Errors; 1994 Olivier Award for Set Design for Hysteria; 1995 Critics' Circle Award for The Kitchen; Olivier Award nomination 2003 and Tony Award nomination 2004 for Best Costume Designer for Bombay Dreams.

Johanna Town (lighting designer)
For the Royal Court includes: My Name is Rachel Corrie, A Girl in a Car with a Man, Food Chain, Under the Whaleback, Terrorism, Plasticine, Fucking Games, I Just Stopped By To See The Man, Mr Kolpert, The Kitchen, Ashes and Sand, Where Do We Live, Via Dolorosa (& Broadway); Shopping & Fucking (with Out of Joint/West End); The Steward of Christendom (with Out of Joint/Broadway).
Other theatre includes: Guantanamo (Tricycle /West End/New York); Macbeth (Out of Joint); Someone Who'll Watch Over Me (Northampton Theatre Royal); How Love is Spelt (Bush); The Permanent Way, She Stoops to Conquer, A Laughing Matter (Out Of Joint/RNT); I.D. (Almeida/BBC 3); Badnuff, Mr Nobody (Soho); A Doll's House (Southwark); Six Degrees of Separation, Ghosts, Misfits, Richard II (Royal Exchange); The Dumb Waiter (Oxford Playhouse); Brassed Off (Liverpool Playhouse/Birmingham Rep); Popcorn, Les Liaisons Dangereuses, Playboy of the Western World (Liverpool Playhouse); Feelgood, Little Malcolm & His Struggle Against the Eunuchs (Hampstead/West End); Rose (RNT/Broadway); Top Girls (West End) and Arabian Nights, Our Lady of Sligo (New York).
Johanna has been Head of Lighting at the Royal Court since 1990.

David Tushingham (translator)
For the Royal Court: Mr Kolpert, Waiting Room Germany, Karate Billy Comes Home, Stranger's House.
Other translations include: Arabian Night by Roland Schimmelpfennig (ATC/Soho Theatre), Jeff Koons (ATC/ICA), Innocence (Accra, Ghana), Adam Geist (Royal Exchange, Manchester), The Actors (Tron, Glasgow), Splinters (BBC Radio 3).
Adaptation: Haroun and the Sea of Stories (RNT).
David Tushingham has worked as a dramaturg in London, Hamburg, Stuttgart, Hanover, Berlin and Vienna. He is currently dramaturg for Theater der Welt 2005 in Stuttgart.

Richard Wilson (director)
Associate Director of the Royal Court.
For the Royal Court: Playing the Victim (co-production with Told by an Idiot), Under the Whaleback, Imprint Young Writers Festival, Where Do We Live, Nightingale and Chase, I Just Stopped By To See The Man, Mr Kolpert (winner of TMA Award for Best Theatre Director), Toast, Four, God's Second in Command, Other Worlds, Heaven and Hell; A Wholly Healthy Glasgow, Women Laughing.
Other theatre includes: Primo (RNT/Hampstead); Four Nights in Knaresborough (New Vic Workshop for the Tricycle); Tom and Clem (tour/West End); Simply Disconnected (Chichester); The Lodger (Hampstead/Royal Exchange, Manchester); Imagine Drowning, President Wilson in Paris, Lenz (Hampstead); Prin (Lyric, Hammersmith); An Inspector Calls (Royal Exchange, Manchester); View of Kabul, Commitments (Bush); Teeth n' Smiles (Oxford Playhouse).
Television includes: Changing Step, A Wholly Healthy Glasgow, Under the Hammer, Remainder Man, Commitments.Richard Wilson has many credits for theatre, film and television as both an actor and a director.

THE ENGLISH STAGE COMPANY AT THE ROYAL COURT

The English Stage Company at the Royal Court opened in 1956 as a subsidised theatre producing new British plays, international plays and some classical revivals.

The first artistic director George Devine aimed to create a writers' theatre, 'a place where the dramatist is acknowledged as the fundamental creative force in the theatre and where the play is more important than the actors, the director, the designer'. The urgent need was to find a contemporary style in which the play, the acting, direction and design are all combined. He believed that 'the battle will be a long one to continue to create the right conditions for writers to work in'.

Devine aimed to discover hard-hitting, uncompromising writers whose plays are stimulating, provocative and exciting'. The Royal Court production of John Osborne's Look Back in Anger in May 1956 is now seen as the decisive starting point of modern British drama and the policy created a new generation of British playwrights. The first wave included John Osborne, Arnold Wesker, John Arden, Ann Jellicoe, N F Simpson and Edward Bond. Early seasons included new international plays by Bertolt Brecht, Eugène Ionesco, Samuel Beckett, Jean-Paul Sartre and Marguerite Duras.

The theatre started with the 400-seat proscenium arch Theatre Downstairs, and in 1969 opened a second theatre, the 60-seat studio Theatre Upstairs. Some productions transfer to the West End, such as Terry Johnson's Hitchcock Blonde, Caryl Churchill's Far Away and Conor McPherson's The Weir. Recent touring productions include Sarah Kane's 4.48 Psychosis (US tour) and Ché Walker's Flesh Wound (Galway Arts Festival). The Royal Court also co-produces plays which have transferred to the West End or toured internationally, such as Conor McPherson's Shining City (with Gate Theatre, Dublin), Sebastian Barry's The Steward of Christendom and Mark Ravenhill's Shopping and Fucking (with Out of Joint), Martin McDonagh's The Beauty Queen Of Leenane (with Druid Theatre), Ayub Khan Din's East is East (with Tamasha).

Since 1994 the Royal Court's artistic policy has again been vigorously directed to finding and producing a new generation of playwrights. The writers include Joe Penhall, Rebecca Prichard, Michael Wynne, Nick Grosso, Judy Upton, Meredith Oakes, Sarah Kane, Anthony Neilson, Judith Johnson, James Stock, Jez Butterworth, Marina Carr, Phyllis Nagy, Simon Block, Martin

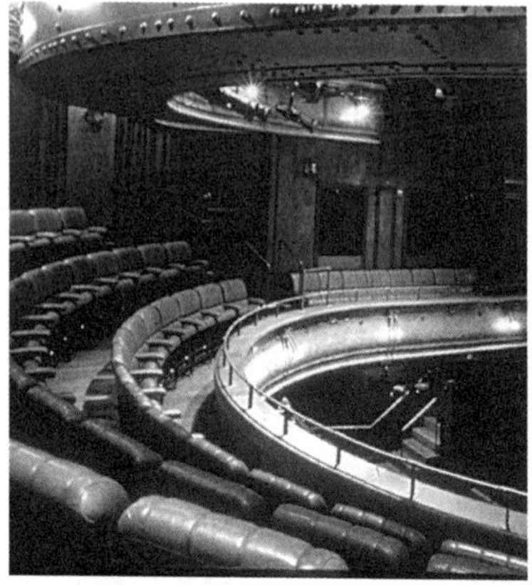

photo: Andy Chopping

McDonagh, Mark Ravenhill, Ayub Khan Din, Tamantha Hammerschlag, Jess Walters, Ché Walker, Conor McPherson, Simon Stephens, Richard Bean, Roy Williams, Gary Mitchell, Mick Mahoney, Rebecca Gilman, Christopher Shinn, Kia Corthron, David Gieselmann, Marius von Mayenburg, David Eldridge, Leo Butler, Zinnie Harris, Grae Cleugh, Roland Schimmelpfennig, Chloe Moss, DeObia Oparei, Enda Walsh, Vassily Sigarev, the Presnyakov Brothers, Marcos Barbosa, Lucy Prebble, John Donnelly, Clare Pollard, Robin French, Elyzabeth Gregory Wilder, Rob Evans and Laura Wade. This expanded programme of new plays has been made possible through the support of A.S.K. Theater Projects and the Skirball Foundation, The Jerwood Charity, the American Friends of the Royal Court Theatre and (in 1994/5 and 1999) in association with the National Theatre Studio.

In recent years there have been record-breaking productions at the box office, with capacity houses for Joe Penhall's Dumb Show, Conor McPherson's Shining City, Roy Williams' Fallout and Terry Johnson's Hitchcock Blonde.

The refurbished theatre in Sloane Square opened in February 2000, with a policy still inspired by the first artistic director George Devine. The Royal Court is an international theatre for new plays and new playwrights, and the work shapes contemporary drama in Britain and overseas.

PROGRAMME SUPPORTERS

The Royal Court (English Stage Company Ltd) receives its principal funding from Arts Council England, London. It is also supported financially by a wide range of private companies, charitable and public bodies, and earns the remainder of its income from the box office and its own trading activities.

The Genesis Foundation supports International Playwrights and the Young Writers' Festival. The Jerwood Charity supports new plays by new playwrights through the Jerwood New Playwrights series.

The Skirball Foundation funds a Playwrights' Programme at the theatre. The Artistic Director's Chair is supported by a lead grant from The Peter Jay Sharp Foundation, contributing to the activities of the Artistic Director's office. Bloomberg Mondays, the Royal Court's reduced price ticket scheme, is supported by Bloomberg. Over the past eight years the BBC has supported the Gerald Chapman Fund for directors.

ROYAL COURT DEVELOPMENT BOARD
Tamara Ingram (Chair)
Jonathan Cameron (Vice Chair)
Timothy Burrill
Anthony Burton
Jonathan Caplan QC
Sindy Caplan
Gavin Casey FCA
Mark Crowdy
Cas Donald
Joseph Fiennes
Amanda Foreman
Joyce Hytner OBE
Gavin Neath
Michael Potter
Kadee Robbins
Mark Robinson
William Russell
Sue Stapely
James L Tanner
Will Turner

PUBLIC FUNDING
Arts Council England, London
British Council
Creative Partnerships London South
London Challenge
Royal Borough of Kensington & Chelsea

TRUSTS AND FOUNDATIONS
American Friends of the Royal Court Theatre
Gerald Chapman Fund
Cowley Charitable Trust
The Dorset Foundation
The Ronald Duncan Literary Foundation
The Foundation for Sport and the Arts
The Foyle Foundation
Francis Finlay Foundation
The Garfield Weston Foundation
Genesis Foundation
The Haberdashers' Company
Jerwood Charity
Lynn Foundation
John Lyon's Charity
The Magowan Family Foundation
The Rayne Foundation
The Royal Victoria Hall Foundation
The Peter Jay Sharp Foundation
Skirball Foundation
The Bruce Wake Charitable Trust
Michael J Zamkow & Sue E Berman Charitable Trust

SPONSORS
Giorgio Armani
Arts & Business New Partners
Barclays
BBC
Bloomberg
City Inn, Westminster
Coutts & Co
Peter Jones

BUSINESS AND MEDIA MEMBERS
Aviva plc
Bloomsbury
Columbia Tristar Films (UK)
Hat Trick Productions
Lazard
Pemberton Greenish
Simons Muirhead & Burton
Slaughter and May

PRODUCTION SYNDICATE
Anonymous
Jonathan & Sindy Caplan
Ms Kay Ellen Consolver
Mrs Philip Donald
Peter & Edna Goldstein
Jack & Linda Keenan
Richard & Robin Landsberger
Kadee Robbins
William & Hilary Russell
Kay Hartenstein Saatchi
Jon & NoraLee Sedmak
Ian & Carol Sellars
James & Victoria Tanner

INDIVIDUAL MEMBERS
Patrons
Anonymous
Dr Bettina Bahlsen
Katie Bradford
Marcus J Burton & Dr M F Ozbigin
Celeste Fenichel
Tom & Simone Fenton
Jack & Linda Keenan
Duncan Matthews QC
Ian & Carol Sellars
Jan & Michael Topham
Richard Wilson OBE

Benefactors
Anonymous
Martha Allfrey
Varian Ayers & Gary Knisely
John & Anoushka Ayton
Lucy Bryn Davies
Jeremy Conway & Nicola Van Gelder
Robyn Durie
Joachim Fleury
Sue and Don Guiney
Tamara Ingram
Peter & Maria Kellner
Barbara Minto
Mr & Mrs Richard Pilosof
Brian D Smith
Sue Stapeley
Amanda Vail
Sir Robert & Lady Wilson
Nick Wheeler

Associates
Act IV
Anonymous
Jeffrey Archer
Brian Boylan
Alan Brodie
Ossi & Paul Burger
Mrs Helena Butler
Lady Cazalet
Carole & Neville Conrad
Margaret Cowper
Andrew Cryer
Linda & Ronald F. Daitz
Zoë Dominic
Kim Dunn
Charlotte & Nick Fraser
Gillian Frumkin
Jacqueline & Jonathan Gestetner
Vivien Goodwin
Judy & Frank Grace
Don & Sue Guiney
P. Hobbs - LTRC
David & Suzie Hyman
Mrs Ellen Josefowitz
David Kaskel & Christopher Teano
Mr & Mrs Tarek Kassem
Carole A. Leng
Lady Lever
Colette & Peter Levy
Mr Watcyn Lewis
David Marks
Nicola McFarland
Gavin & Ann Neath
Mr & Mrs Michael Orr
Pauline Pinder
William Poeton CBE & Barbara Poeton
Jan & Michael Potter
Jeremy Priestley
Beverley Rider
John Ritchie
Lois Sieff OBE
Gail Steele
Will Turner
Anthony Wigram

THE AMERICAN FRIENDS OF THE ROYAL COURT THEATRE

AFRCT supports the mission of the Royal Court and are primarily focused on raising funds to enable the theatre to produce new work by emerging American writers. Since this not-for-profit organisation was founded in 1997, AFRCT has contributed to ten productions. It has also supported the participation of young artists in the Royal Court's acclaimed International Residency.

If you would like to support the ongoing work of the Royal Court, please contact the Development Department on 020 7565 5050.

Founders
Francis Finlay
Amanda Foreman & Jonathan Barton
Monica Gerard-Sharp & Ali Wambold
Blythe Masters
Laura Pels
Ben Rauch & Margaret Scott
Mr & Mrs Gerald Schoenfeld

Patrons
Catherine Curran
William & Ursula Fairbairn
Francis H Goldwyn
Mr & Mrs Richard Grand
Sahra Lese
Imelda Liddiard

Benefactors
Rachael Bail
David Day & John Drummond
Jeff & Cynthia Penney
Timothy Runion & Vipul Nishawala
Mika Sterling
Mr & Mrs Robert G Donnalley

Members
Harry Brown & Richard Walsh
Georgiana Ellis
Nancy Flinn
Jennifer R Gardner
Sharon King Hope
Nancy Lamb
Rochelle Ohrstom
Evelyn Renold
Roberta Schneidermann
Patricia Shea
David & Patricia Smalley

Corporations & Foundations
American Express Company
The Blessing Way Foundation
The Edmond de Rothschild Foundation
The Howard Gilman Foundation
The Lone Pine Foundation
The Magowan Family Foundation
The Patchwork Charitable Foundation
Proskauer Rose LLP
The Laura Pels Foundation
The Shubert Organization
The Sy Syms Foundation
Union Pacific Corporation

American Friends Development Director
Timothy Runion
Tel: 001 212 946 5724

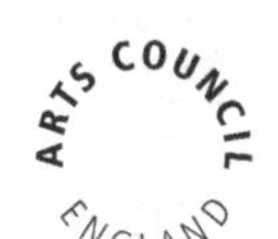

AWARDS FOR ROYAL COURT

Jez Butterworth won the 1995 George Devine Award, the Writers' Guild New Writer of the Year Award, the Evening Standard Award for Most Promising Playwright and the Olivier Award for Best Comedy for Mojo.

The Royal Court was the overall winner of the 1995 Prudential Award for the Arts for creativity, excellence, innovation and accessibility. The Royal Court Theatre Upstairs won the 1995 Peter Brook Empty Space Award for innovation and excellence in theatre.

Michael Wynne won the 1996 Meyer-Whitworth Award for The Knocky. Martin McDonagh won the 1996 George Devine Award, the 1996 Writers' Guild Best Fringe Play Award, the 1996 Critics' Circle Award and the 1996 Evening Standard Award for Most Promising Playwright for The Beauty Queen of Leenane. Marina Carr won the 19th Susan Smith Blackburn Prize (1996/7) for Portia Coughlan. Conor McPherson won the 1997 George Devine Award, the 1997 Critics' Circle Award and the 1997 Evening Standard Award for Most Promising Playwright for The Weir. Ayub Khan Din won the 1997 Writers' Guild Awards for Best West End Play and New Writer of the Year and the 1996 John Whiting Award for East is East (co-production with Tamasha).

Martin McDonagh's The Beauty Queen of Leenane (co-production with Druid Theatre Company) won four 1998 Tony Awards including Garry Hynes for Best Director. Eugene Ionesco's The Chairs (co-production with Theatre de Complicite) was nominated for six Tony awards. David Hare won the 1998 Time Out Live Award for Outstanding Achievement and six awards in New York including the Drama League, Drama Desk and New York Critics Circle Award for Via Dolorosa. Sarah Kane won the 1998 Arts Foundation Fellowship in Playwriting. Rebecca Prichard won the 1998 Critics' Circle Award for Most Promising Playwright for Yard Gal (co-production with Clean Break).

Conor McPherson won the 1999 Olivier Award for Best New Play for The Weir. The Royal Court won the 1999 ITI Award for Excellence in International Theatre. Sarah Kane's Cleansed was judged Best Foreign Language Play in 1999 by Theater Heute in Germany. Gary Mitchell won the 1999 Pearson Best Play Award for Trust. Rebecca Gilman was joint winner of the 1999 George Devine Award and won the 1999 Evening Standard Award for Most Promising Playwright for The Glory of Living.

In 1999, the Royal Court won the European theatre prize New Theatrical Realities, presented at Taormina Arte in Sicily, for its efforts in recent years in discovering and producing the work of young British dramatists.

Roy Williams and Gary Mitchell were joint winners of the George Devine Award 2000 for Most Promising Playwright for Lift Off and The Force of Change respectively. At the Barclays Theatre Awards 2000 presented by the TMA, Richard Wilson won the Best Director Award for David Gieselmann's Mr Kolpert and Jeremy Herbert won the Best Designer Award for Sarah Kane's 4.48 Psychosis. Gary Mitchell won the Evening Standard's Charles Wintour Award 2000 for Most Promising Playwright for The Force of Change. Stephen Jeffreys' I Just Stopped by to See the Man won an AT&T: On Stage Award 2000.

David Eldridge's Under the Blue Sky won the Time Out Live Award 2001 for Best New Play in the West End. Leo Butler won the George Devine Award 2001 for Most Promising Playwright for Redundant. Roy Williams won the Evening Standard's Charles Wintour Award 2001 for Most Promising Playwright for Clubland. Grae Cleugh won the 2001 Olivier Award for Most Promising Playwright for Fucking Games. Richard Bean was joint winner of the George Devine Award 2002 for Most Promising Playwright for Under the Whaleback. Caryl Churchill won the 2002 Evening Standard Award for Best New Play for A Number. Vassily Sigarev won the 2002 Evening Standard Charles Wintour Award for Most Promising Playwright for Plasticine. Ian MacNeil won the 2002 Evening Standard Award for Best Design for A Number and Plasticine. Peter Gill won the 2002 Critics' Circle Award for Best New Play for The York Realist (English Touring Theatre). Ché Walker won the 2003 George Devine Award for Most Promising Playwright for Flesh Wound. Lucy Prebble won the 2003 Critics' Circle Award and the 2004 George Devine Award for Most Promising Playwright, and the TMA Theatre Award 2004 for Best New Play for The Sugar Syndrome. Linda Bassett won the 2004 TMA Theatre Award for Best Actress (for Leo Butler's Lucky Dog).

ROYAL COURT BOOKSHOP

The Royal Court bookshop offers a range of contemporary plays and publications on the theory and practice of modern drama. The staff specialise in assisting with the selection of audition monologues and scenes.
Royal Court playtexts from past and present productions cost £2.
The Bookshop is situated in the downstairs ROYAL COURT BAR AND FOOD.
Monday–Friday 3–10pm, Saturday 2.30–10pm
For information tel: 020 7565 5024
or email: bookshop@royalcourttheatre.com

FOR THE ROYAL COURT

Royal Court Theatre, Sloane Square, London SW1W 8AS
Tel: 020 7565 5050 Fax: 020 7565 5001
info@royalcourttheatre.com
www.royalcourttheatre.com

Artistic Director **Ian Rickson**
Associate Director International **Elyse Dodgson**
Associate Director **Marianne Elliott**+
Associate Director Casting **Lisa Makin**
Associate Directors* **Stephen Daldry, Ramin Gray, James Macdonald, Katie Mitchell, Max Stafford-Clark, Richard Wilson**
Literary Manager **Graham Whybrow**
Pearson Playwright **Lucy Prebble**†
Literary Associate **Terry Johnson***
Voice Associate **Patsy Rodenburg***
Casting Deputy **Amy Ball**
International Associate **Tiffany Watt-Smith**
International Administrator **Chris James**
Artistic Assistant **Polly Wines**

Production Manager **Paul Handley**
Deputy Production Manager **Sue Bird**
Production Assistant **Sarah Davies**
Facilities Manager **Fran McElroy**
Head of Lighting **Johanna Town**
Lighting Deputy **Trevor Wallace**
Lighting Assistants **Nicki Brown**
Lighting Board Operator **Kelli Marston**
Head of Stage **Martin Riley**
Stage Deputy **Steven Stickler**
Stage Chargehand **Daniel Lockett**
Head of Sound **Ian Dickinson**
Sound Deputy **Emma Laxton**
Head of Costume **Iona Kenrick**
Costume Deputy **Jackie Orton**

YOUNG WRITERS PROGRAMME
Associate Director **Ola Animashawun**
Administrator **Nina Lyndon**
Outreach Worker **Lucy Dunkerley**
Education Officer **Emily McLaughlin**
Writers Tutor **Simon Stephens***

General Manager **Diane Borger**
Administrator **Ushi Bagga**
Finance Director **Sarah Preece**
Finance Officer **Rachel Harrison***
Finance Officer **Martin Wheeler**
Finance Manager **Helen Perryer***

Head of Marketing **Penny Mills**
Head of Press **Ewan Thomson**
Marketing Officer **Alix Hearn**
Press Officer **Lyndsay Roberts**
Box Office Manager **Neil Grutchfield**
Deputy Box Office Manager **Valli Dakshinamurthi**
Assistant Box Office Manager **Glen Bowman**
Box Office Sales Operators **Louise Kelly, Steven Kuleshnyk, Hannah McCarthy**
Press and Marketing Intern **Megan Wildebour**

Head of Development **Helen Salmon**
Trusts and Foundations Manager **Nicky Jones**
Development Manager **Leona Felton**
Development Officer **Natalie Moss**
Development Intern **Hazel Vidler**

Theatre Manager **Elizabeth Brown**
Deputy Theatre Manager **Bobbie Stokes**
Front of House Manager **Nathalie Meghriche**
Duty House Managers* **Charlie Revell, David Duchin, Polly Wines**
Bookshop Manager **Simon David**
Assistant Bookshop Manager **Edin Suljic***
Bookshop Assistant* **Nicki Welburn**
Stage Door/Reception **Simon David, Jon Hunter, Tyrone Lucas, Paul Lovegrove**

Thanks to all of our box office assistants and ushers.

+ The Associate Director post is supported by the BBC through the Gerald Chapman Fund.
† This theatre has the support of the Pearson Playwright's Scheme sponsored by Pearson plc.
* Part-time.

ENGLISH STAGE COMPANY

President
Sir John Mortimer CBE QC

Vice President
Dame Joan Plowright CBE

Honorary Council
Sir Richard Eyre CBE
Alan Grieve CBE

Council
Chairman **Anthony Burton**
Vice Chairwoman **Liz Calder**

Members
Judy Daish
Graham Devlin
Joyce Hytner OBE
Tamara Ingram
Stephen Jeffreys
Phyllida Lloyd
James Midgley
Edward Miliband
Sophie Okonedo
Katharine Viner

THE WOMAN BEFORE

First published in this translation in 2005 by Oberon Books Ltd
521 Caledonian Road, London N7 9RH
Tel: 020 7607 3637 / Fax: 020 7607 3629
e-mail: oberon.books@btconnect.com
www.oberonbooks.com

A catalogue record for this book is available from the British Library.

ISBN: 1 84002 572 7

Cover photo: Jay Clark / Research Studios

Printed in Great Britain by Antony Rowe Ltd, Chippenham

Characters

FRANK
mid forties

CLAUDIA
his wife

ROMY VOGTLÄNDER

ANDI
Frank and Claudia's son

TINA
Andi's girlfriend

The shifts in time at the beginning of each new scene need to be made clear, either through written signs, voiceover or some other means.

The generous hallway of an old-fashioned apartment. Four doors lead off the hall: double front doors, a door to the bathroom, a door to the son's room and a door to the parents' bedroom. Perhaps a corridor with one more door leading to the living-room and kitchen. Lots of space. Filled packing-cases already lie in the hallway – there are no items of furniture or pictures left.

1

FRANK is standing by the front door, which is closed. His wife CLAUDIA comes out of the bathroom wearing a bathrobe and with a towel round her head.

CLAUDIA: Who are you talking to?

FRANK: Me?

CLAUDIA: Yeah, who are you talking to?

FRANK: Er – nobody. Who's there to talk to –

CLAUDIA: I thought I heard someone talking – you were talking to somebody –

FRANK: No – why?

CLAUDIA: Because I heard voices.

FRANK: Voices –

CLAUDIA: Yes, voices –

FRANK: But you were in the bathroom –

CLAUDIA: I know –

FRANK: You know what that is – voices in the pipes, from other floors –

CLAUDIA: No – I'm taking about voices from out here, in the hall.

FRANK: Voices – here –

CLAUDIA: Yes, voices – here in the hall.

Brief pause.

FRANK: There's no one here.

Brief pause.

CLAUDIA: But there was someone.

Brief pause.

FRANK: There's nobody here.

She opens the front door. ROMY VOGTLÄNDER is standing right in the doorway. She's wearing a short coat.

Pause.

CLAUDIA: Who's that?

Silence.

Who is that?

Brief pause.

FRANK: That –

Brief pause.

That is Romy Vogtländer,

Brief pause.

That's Romy Vogtländer, who I've not seen for twenty-four years.

Brief pause.

CLAUDIA: Why didn't you tell me this woman was standing outside the door?

Pause.

Why didn't you tell me that?

Brief pause.

Why are you lying to me –

Brief pause.

FRANK: I'm just as surprised as you are to see her there.

Brief pause.

ROMY: Twenty-four years ago this man was the love of my life.

Brief pause.

We were lovers then.

Brief pause.

And we still are now.

Brief pause.

CLAUDIA: What?

ROMY: Him and me – we were lovers then and we still are now.

CLAUDIA slaps her husband's face and slams the door in front of ROMY VOGTLÄNDER.

2

Ten minutes earlier. The empty hallway. Shower noises from the bathroom. A ring at the bell.

FRANK enters, goes to the intercom.

FRANK: Yep?

Nothing.

Hello? Hello?

Nothing.

Hello?

He exits. Another ring. He returns, picks up the phone on the intercom.

Hello?

Nothing. He hangs up, exits once more. There is a knock at the door. He pauses. Silence. Another knock. He goes back to the door.

Hello? Who is it?

More knocking.

Hello?

Silence.

He opens the door suddenly. In the doorway there's a woman in a short coat.

FRANK: Yes?

Silence.

What is it?

Silence.

Listen –

ROMY: I've been looking for you – you weren't easy to find –

FRANK: Yeah – right.

He closes the door but stands there motionless.

Pause.

A knock. He opens the door again.

Listen, please –

The sound of the shower in the bathroom stops.

ROMY: You – you don't recognize me –

FRANK: Recognize you,

Laughs.

I don't, recognize you, no, sorry –

He's about to shut the door again.

ROMY: It's me, Romy, – Romy Vogtländer.

Brief pause.

But if you don't recognize me then you really should shut the door again.

FRANK: Romy Vogtländer –

ROMY: You don't even recognize me.

FRANK: Romy – Romy Vogtländer…

ROMY: You know now –

FRANK: Yes –

ROMY: For one whole summer we were lovers –

FRANK: Romy Vogtländer…

ROMY: Twenty-four years ago.

FRANK: Romy…that was.

Brief pause.

We were seventeen then.

ROMY: Seventeen, that's right, I was seventeen, and you were twenty, and you swore that you'd love me for ever.

He laughs out loud.

FRANK: Yeah –

ROMY: You laugh about it –

And I swore too. That I'd love you forever.

Brief pause.

Remember?

FRANK: Yeah – right.

ROMY: Now I've come to hold you to that promise.

Pause.

FRANK: What?

ROMY: Now I've come to hold you to that promise. I'm here to remind you of the promise you made –

FRANK: What promise –

ROMY: The promise that you'll love me for ever, that's what you said.

Pause.

FRANK: But – but –

Brief pause.

I was nineteen.

ROMY: Twenty.

FRANK: Nineteen, twenty – it makes no difference –

Brief pause.

What do you want?

Brief pause.

ROMY: You – what else could I want.

I've come to remind you.

FRANK: Remind me –

ROMY: That we will love each other for all time – that's what you said.

He considers. The sound of the lock of a bathroom door that is about to open. He shuts the front door in ROMY VOGTLÄNDER's face. Holds his breath. CLAUDIA enters from the bathroom in a bathrobe with a towel around her head.

CLAUDIA: Who are you talking to?

FRANK: Me?

CLAUDIA: Yeah, who are you talking to?

FRANK: Er – nobody. Who's there to talk to –

CLAUDIA: I thought I heard someone talking – you were talking to somebody –

FRANK: No – why?

CLAUDIA: Because I heard voices.

FRANK: Voices –

CLAUDIA: Yes, voices –

FRANK: But you were in the bathroom –

CLAUDIA: I know –

FRANK: You know what that is – voices in the pipes, from other floors –

CLAUDIA: No – I'm taking about voices from out here, in the hall.

FRANK: Voices – here –

CLAUDIA: Yes, voices – here in the hall.

Brief pause.

FRANK: There isn't anyone here.

Brief pause.

CLAUDIA: But there was someone.

Brief pause.

FRANK: There's nobody here.

She opens the front door. ROMY VOGTLÄNDER is standing right in the doorway. She's wearing a short coat.

Pause.

CLAUDIA: Who's that?

Silence.

CLAUDIA: Who is that?

Brief pause.

FRANK: That –

Brief pause.

That is Romy Vogtländer,

Brief pause.

That's Romy Vogtländer, who I've not seen for twenty-four years.

Brief pause.

CLAUDIA: Why didn't you tell me this woman was standing outside the door?

Pause.

Why didn't you tell me that?

Brief pause.

Why are you lying to me –

Brief pause.

FRANK: I'm just as surprised as you are to see her there.

Brief pause.

ROMY: Twenty-four years ago this man was the love of my life.

Brief pause.

We were lovers then.

Brief pause.

And we still are now.

Brief pause.

CLAUDIA: What?

ROMY: Him and me – we were lovers then and we still are now.

CLAUDIA slaps FRANK across the face. Slams the door.

3

In front of the building, later.

TINA: Andi and me, it's a warm evening, our last one, – the autumn sun's already low and we –

We don't want to go home – we can't leave each other, but tomorrow he and his parents are going to move, a long way away. We love each other. He's my boyfriend, my first boyfriend. I don't want him to go.

But it's all set – his parents have got everything packed, these are our final hours, we sit on the bank in front of the building and don't know what to say – I love you, I'll never forget you, stay with me, what's going to happen, you –

We sit at the top of the bank, just like we always do, like we have so many times, and see a woman in a raincoat who comes and rings at the door. What's going to happen to us?

I don't know, haven't got a clue.

I hold his hand or he holds mine, we sit there, not knowing what's next.

4

A few minutes earlier. Inside.

CLAUDIA: What?

ROMY: Him and me – we were lovers then and we still are now.

CLAUDIA slaps FRANK in the face and slams the door shut in front of ROMY VOGTLÄNDER.

Brief pause.

CLAUDIA: How – how can you do this to me –

FRANK: What – do what to you? I haven't done anything –

CLAUDIA: You lied to me –

FRANK: How was I supposed to explain there's this woman standing on our doorstep?

CLAUDIA: This woman – evidently the great love of your youth –

FRANK: It was twenty-four years ago –

CLAUDIA: And I get to hear about for the first time today –

FRANK: I'd completely forgotten her, to begin with I didn't even recognize her –

CLAUDIA: Then tell her that!

FRANK: What –

CLAUDIA: Tell her you'd forgotten her, that you didn't even recognize her, tell that to her! Instead of standing here listening to her tell me to my face that you and she are lovers –

FRANK: It wasn't my fault, –

CLAUDIA: No? Whose was it then?

FRANK: I can't help it, all I did was open the door –

CLAUDIA: And lie to me –

FRANK: What do you mean, lie, I couldn't –

CLAUDIA flings the door open again. ROMY VOGTLÄNDER is still standing there.

CLAUDIA: (*Shouts.*) What now?

Brief pause.

What happens now? What are we going to do now?

ROMY: Now –

Brief pause.

CLAUDIA: Yes, now –

ROMY: Now – now Frank's going to remember what he once promised me, that our love would never end.

CLAUDIA: I see –

ROMY: He's going to remember that and then he'll either ask me in and send you away –

CLAUDIA: You need help – .

ROMY: Or he'll put his coat on and come with me – if we can't stay here because of you. It's quite clear. I've been thinking about this moment for a long time.

CLAUDIA: Only none of that's going to happen; he's not going to do any of those things: no one's going to invite you in, nor is Frank going to send me away as you hope, nor is he going to put on his coat and leave here with you.

ROMY: Isn't he? How can you be so sure? How are you going to know –

CLAUDIA: Me?

Brief pause.

– You're right, absolutely right, it's true –

Brief pause.

he will leave here – but with me, not you.

Brief pause.

ROMY: What – with you –

CLAUDIA: It's purely a coincidence you managed to catch us at all. We're moving – tomorrow, after nineteen years.

Brief pause.

ROMY: Where would you want to go with her now that I'm back?

CLAUDIA: Far away – a long, long way from here.

ROMY: Where?

CLAUDIA: More than half our belongings are already on the high seas, the rest are being packed today and collected tomorrow lunchtime. You've left it rather late –

Brief pause.

ROMY: And you're not saying anything – you can't do that, let all that go without saying a word.

You've got to say something. You must speak.

Brief pause.

FRANK: It's true.

ROMY: What is, what's true, tell me –

FRANK: It's true, Claudia and I have been together for almost twenty years, we're married, we've got a son who's almost grown up.

ROMY: (*Forcefully.*) How – how can she have your child –

FRANK: – and we're leaving here tomorrow.

Brief pause.

Being together once doesn't bind us for ever.

ROMY: Yes it does, that's exactly what it does; you said so.

Brief pause.

You even sang it for me; can't you remember the song? Can't you remember the song you sang for me?

FRANK: (*Interrupts her.*) It doesn't matter what I might have said twenty-four years ago – it doesn't count any more. We're not lovers, we were for a summer or two, maybe, at the most but Claudia and I have known each other for twenty years.

CLAUDIA: During which as far as I can recall he has never sung anything –

ROMY: Like I said, she doesn't even know you –

CLAUDIA: I am the mother of his child – I have accompanied this man through every decisive phase of his life, I know every one of his thoughts, every gesture, every step, just as well as he knows me –

ROMY: Knows! You might know her, but love – for the last twenty-four years you've loved no one but me, the only woman for you –

CLAUDIA: That is enough. Tell her you'd completely forgotten her – at first you didn't even recognize her.

ROMY: You can't; you can't send me away, it's impossible. This is a bad dream – it'll be over soon.

FRANK: No – it's true.

ROMY: I'm having a nightmare but I'm going to wake up in a minute

Brief pause.

– and in a minute when I open my eyes, you'll bend down over me, right beside my face and you'll ask me tenderly: how are you? Are you alright? And I, I'll say: I knew it, you've brought me back at last. And then we'll kiss.

CLAUDIA: I promise you: he is not going to bring you back, he is not going to say anything to you – and he won't kiss you.

Brief pause.

Now I'm going to shut the door.

ROMY: I'll see you – see you later.

5

Later.

TINA: And then, a few minutes later, the woman in the raincoat leaves again, she's agitated, confused, you can tell, she takes a few steps, stops, turns round, turns back again and takes a few more steps –

I can't explain why, but I pick up a stone.

I pick up a stone and throw it at that woman. I miss.

I hear the stone land, smash on the pavement.

I pick up another stone and throw that but I miss her again. The stone bangs on the pavement. The woman stops and looks round. She's puzzled by these stones bouncing around but she doesn't see us even though she looks straight up in our direction. And then Andi lets go of my hand and he picks a stone up and throws it at her – neither of us knows why. He throws the stone just as she's about to walk on.

6

Meanwhile: in the flat. FRANK and CLAUDIA. Both packing in silence. He is busy assembling a new packing-case. CLAUDIA is now dressed. She drags a full box on stage from out of the living-room.

CLAUDIA: What's in this box?

FRANK: I dunno.

CLAUDIA: Didn't you pack this one?

FRANK: Might have done.

CLAUDIA: I didn't pack it.

FRANK: Must have been me then –

CLAUDIA: But you don't know what's in it.

FRANK: I dunno.

Brief pause.

CLAUDIA: It's too full.

FRANK: Too full? It's closed isn't it?

CLAUDIA: It's too heavy. Soon as you pick it up, the bottom'll fall out.

Brief pause.

How many times have I said – if you put too much in these boxes, the bottom's going to fall out. I don't know how many times I must have asked you.

FRANK: I know, you say it every time, every single time I pack one of these boxes, and then you go and pack them again which is why it takes us twice as long and yet so far the bottom hasn't fallen out of any of them, not even one of the ones I packed.

He is annoyed and walks up to the box which she just dragged into the hall.

He grabs hold of it in order to put it on top of the other packing-cases.

The bottom falls out of this packing-case and its contents fall on the floor.

CLAUDIA: (*Accusingly.*) No!

FRANK: What the hell is that –

A pile of plastic bags with things inside have burst out of the packing-case.

CLAUDIA: The pebbles! The pebbles with the holes in!

FRANK: Well I didn't do that – I've not touched those pebbles in years. Didn't even know we still had them.

CLAUDIA has taken a stone out of one of the bags.

CLAUDIA: Look –

She looks through the tiny hole in the pebble.

If you look through the hole you can see the future, that's what they say.

FRANK: Or the past – depending which way round you've got it.

CLAUDIA: Yeah?

She takes a quick look at both sides of the stone.

FRANK: Why did you put them in separate bags –

CLAUDIA: Why? Look –

She holds up the bag.

– take a good look at this bag.

He takes a moment to think of reading what's written on the bag. The bag has a picture of the Eiffel Tower on it.

FRANK: No!

CLAUDIA: See where it's from?

FRANK: You –

Brief pause.

You kept that all this time – you're not telling me you've kept that for nineteen years –

CLAUDIA: Yes – yes I have –

Brief pause.

FRANK: Come here –

CLAUDIA: No!

FRANK: Come here!

CLAUDIA: No! We've got to keep on packing.

FRANK: Come on –

Brief pause. She goes to him. They hug.

CLAUDIA: (*In his arms.*) There are only two possible explanations for you never telling me about her.

FRANK: Stop it, just enjoy the fact she's gone.

CLAUDIA: Either she really meant nothing to you – and you'd simply forgotten her –

FRANK fondles her.

CLAUDIA: Or she meant a great deal to you indeed –

She extricates herself from his arms.

And that's why you never mentioned her. You kept her a secret from me.

She eyes him critically.

FRANK: I'd completely forgotten her. Even now I can't remember properly.

CLAUDIA: But you told her –

FRANK: What?

CLAUDIA: That –

FRANK: No – that was – that was the words to some song – I don't know, I can't even remember –

Brief pause.

CLAUDIA: So you might have told her that then – you just can't remember.

Brief pause.

Poor woman –

7

The lock shatters. The front door flies open. Brief pause.

ANDI – FRANK and CLAUDIA's son – breaks in. He's out of breath, as if in shock, unable to speak. In his arms he's carrying the dead body of ROMY VOGTLÄNDER, still wearing her raincoat.

ANDI: Help –

CLAUDIA: What –

FRANK: What's –

ANDI: She was outside, on the pavement, lying there –

Brief pause.

FRANK: Romy –

ANDI: She's dead –

FRANK: Dead?

ANDI: Yes, dead – she was lying there dead on the pavement in front of the house.

Brief pause.

CLAUDIA: This woman – dead – why couldn't you just leave her there?

Brief pause.

ANDI: What?

CLAUDIA: Why didn't you leave her there?

ANDI: Leave her? The woman's dead!

CLAUDIA: Yes –

ANDI: I couldn't –

FRANK: He couldn't –

CLAUDIA: Why not, what are we supposed to do with her?

Brief pause.

What are we supposed to do with her body in here? Take her back –

ANDI: Back outside? I'm supposed to go down and put her back on the pavement? No way!

CLAUDIA: Dead or alive, that woman's not coming into my home.

ANDI: I can't take her back again –

CLAUDIA: Why not, you're the one who brought her.

Brief pause.

ANDI: (*It bursts out of him.*) I killed her!

FRANK: You did what?

CLAUDIA: What are you talking about –

ANDI: I killed her –

CLAUDIA tries to close the smashed door but it is so badly broken that it always stays a little open, even force does no good.

FRANK: Put her – put her down over here –

ANDI lies the dead woman's body down on a couple of cardboard boxes.

CLAUDIA: This can't –

ANDI: I don't understand how it could have happened –

FRANK: What? What happened?

ANDI: Tina and me, today's our last day, the sun's already setting and then she, this woman, walks out of the building and I can't say why but she annoys us, something about her, the way she walks, I dunno what it is, we're restless, she pisses us off, we both feel it at the same time and then Tina grabs a stone and throws it at her, she misses, twice, she's too far away, no chance of hitting her, I think, and I throw one at her too but the stone, it's like it's drawn towards her, it flies straight at her just as she turns away and gets her bang on the head. She falls down and doesn't get up again.

Brief pause.

What have I done?

Pause.

That one moment, throwing that one stone's going to cost me my whole life.

Silence. Nobody knows what to say.

The mother hugs her son. His father turns to the dead woman's body.

FRANK: She's alive!

ANDI: What?

FRANK: Yeah, she's breathing,

Brief pause.

it's shallow, but she's breathing –

CLAUDIA: She's alive –

FRANK: She's just passed out – the stone must have knocked her unconscious –

Brief pause.

You didn't kill her.

Brief pause.

ANDI: I didn't –

FRANK: But we can't leave her lying here like this – if she's got concussion she ought to be in the dark.

CLAUDIA: Where are we going to put her –

ANDI: On the sofa –

CLAUDIA: The sofa's gone –

ANDI: Gone –

CLAUDIA: It's been shipped, gone, like practically all the furniture –

FRANK: Well she can't stay where she is – who knows how long it'll take for her to come round –

ANDI: Then put her in your bed –

CLAUDIA: Never. There is no way she is ever going in our bed –

FRANK: What about your bed – let's put her in your bed.

ANDI: My bed – I – if she goes in my – what am I going to do,

Brief pause.

Tina's coming round again later, for the last time –

CLAUDIA: You don't have to meet here do you –

ANDI: But –

Brief pause.

We can't go to hers, her dad hates me.

Brief pause.

CLAUDIA: Go to the cinema – there are so many places –

ANDI: And after that? I'm not spending the night in my bed next to her!

Silence.

FRANK: You can't –

ANDI: I won't!

FRANK: You can't –

ANDI: I won't do it! I wish I'd never brought her up here –

ANDI exits angrily.

FRANK and CLAUDIA remain with the unconscious ROMY VOGTLÄNDER.

FRANK: Let's carry her over –

CLAUDIA: You carry her –

FRANK: I can't carry her by myself –

CLAUDIA: Can't you? Is she too heavy? I'm sure you could before –

What's that?

FRANK: What?

CLAUDIA: That – on the floor – there

Is that blood?

FRANK: Blood?

CLAUDIA: Yes –

FRANK: Where?

CLAUDIA: There, on the floor –

FRANK: You're right – there is a stain there, I hadn't noticed that.

It's –

He examines the stain.

It is blood – she's bleeding –

CLAUDIA: Where?

FRANK: I can't see anything –

CLAUDIA: Then look –

He briefly examines the woman lying on top of the cardboard boxes.

FRANK: Aren't any wounds –

CLAUDIA: The wound must be hidden – under her clothes or her hair – have a proper look. You can touch her – it's not like it's the first time.

FRANK: Why don't you do it?

CLAUDIA: Me? No way. I am not touching that body.

He examines ROMY VOGTLÄNDER's body under CLAUDIA's watchful eyes.

After a moment –

Well?

FRANK: Nothing –

CLAUDIA: Does her body still feel the same as before?

FRANK breaks off, looks at CLAUDIA. Then carries on.

Well? Does she feel the same? Can you remember now? Are the memories coming back?

FRANK: Here it is –

He shows the blood on his hand to prove the point.

It's here – under the hairline – there's a cut.

Brief pause.

We'd better bandage it –

CLAUDIA: Bandage –

FRANK: Yeah – look for some bandages – she's still bleeding –

CLAUDIA makes a hopeless effort to open some of the boxes –

CLAUDIA: How am I supposed to find bandages now – everything's packed!

FRANK: I'll pop down to the car then –

CLAUDIA: You –

FRANK: Just down to the car –

CLAUDIA: And what am I going to do?

FRANK: Stay here with her – till I come back –

CLAUDIA: No – I'm not staying alone with her! You can't leave me on my own with her – what am I supposed to do if she wakes up – don't forget what I said to her!

FRANK: Then you go and I'll stay with her.

CLAUDIA: You'll stay with her –

I'm supposed to leave you here with her alone –

FRANK: Someone's got to go –

CLAUDIA: Why don't we shake her awake and prop her up outside the door –

FRANK: In that state – we're lucky she's not dead.

CLAUDIA: Maybe that would have been the best –

FRANK: Go to the car and get the sodding bandages –

CLAUDIA: Why don't we both go –

FRANK: (*Increasing in volume.*) You can't leave her lying here on her own.

Just go – !

CLAUDIA exits hesitantly.

8

FRANK and ROMY VOGTLÄNDER. He sits next to the woman who is lying on the cardboard boxes, holding her head, as he has done the whole time. Nothing, except this image. He looks at the woman. He looks straight ahead. She opens her eyes and looks at him for a long time without him noticing. Then:

FRANK: How are you? Are you alright?

ROMY: I knew it, you've brought me back at last. At last –

FRANK: No –

ROMY: Yes, you have,

Brief pause.

Or else I wouldn't be here –

She sinks back into unconsciousness. Pause. He still sits on the box holding her head.

Then he stands up, still holding her and carries her into ANDI's room.

Empty stage. His wife returns hurriedly with the bandages.

CLAUDIA: Here –

Nobody there. She stands alone in the hallway.

9

Later that night, around half past three. The empty hallway. ROMY VOGTLÄNDER, her head bandaged, emerges in the semi-darkness from the son's room. She stands motionless in the hallway. Then she sits down on one of the cardboard boxes. Silence.

ANDI comes in through the front door which has been provisionally propped shut with two or three cardboard boxes piled one on top of the other. He pushes the boxes to one side with the panel of the door. This makes the top one fall over. Some old toys and matchbox cars spill out onto the floor. The son switches the light on, but looks only at the floor –

ANDI: My box – it would have to be my box.

He starts putting his things back into the box.

Why does my box have to be the one that's –

ROMY: Don't be alarmed –

ANDI: (*Shocked.*) Ah –

Brief pause. Stops clearing up.

Where are my parents –

ROMY: Asleep –

Brief pause.

ANDI: And you?

ROMY: I'm awake.

ANDI: Yeah –

ROMY: And you?

ANDI: I'm awake too.

ROMY: Where've you been?

ANDI: Outside –

ROMY: It's half past three. Aren't you tired?

ANDI: No –

ROMY: Don't you want to lie down?

ANDI: No, no –

Brief pause.

Aren't you tired?

ROMY: No –

Brief pause.

ANDI: You can have the bed.

ROMY: I can?

Brief pause.

But it's your bed –

ANDI: Yeah – still.

Pause. Neither of them says anything. ANDI suddenly turns to the wall and puts a tag – a written sign – on the wall with a strong black pen he takes out of his trouser pocket. Then he turns back to face ROMY VOGTLÄNDER and looks at her. Pause.

ROMY: What's that?

ANDI: My tag.

ROMY: Your tag – what kind of tag –

ANDI: My tag – it's like my name – it's mine.

ROMY: Why do you do that?

ANDI: It's my tag – anyone who sees it knows I've been here.

ROMY: I see –

ANDI: Yeah.

ROMY: But who's going to see it –

ANDI: What –

ROMY: See that you were here.

Pause.

ANDI: I dunno.

Brief pause.

We'll be out of here tomorrow.

ROMY: Then they're bound to repaint here.

Brief pause.

ANDI: Still – I was here.

10

TINA: We can't go to his because the woman he hit on the head with a stone's there and we can't go to mine because my dad hates him. My dad says he's got shifty eyes.

We meet as it's getting dark at the top of the bank like we always do, and then we go to the cinema.

The film tells the story of a woman who's got to find Pandora's Box before it falls into the hands of a man who's going to use it to threaten the whole world. The chase extends over several continents. It leads them from Greece to England and then on to Russia, China and finally Africa, the birthplace of humanity.

We follow our heroine in submarines, on motorbikes, in jeeps, by parachute, ship, on horseback, suspended from helicopters.

Then we get the bus home. It's half past eleven and we're back at the top of the bank again, outside. It's cold and I'm not dressed for it but it's still too early to go to mine. By half past twelve it's so cold I can't stand it any more and we go to mine.

I go in the front door, Andi waits down in the garden by my window.

Everything in the house is dark, everything's quiet, my parents are asleep upstairs, on the first floor.

My room's in the basement. Andi climbs in through the window not making a sound. Everything's quiet.

We lie side by side in my narrow bed in the dark in silence. No music. Above us and around us – like an ancient mausoleum – the house, a small bathroom, my room and the cellar downstairs, the kitchen and the living-room on the ground floor, upstairs my parents' bedroom and a second bathroom.

Just as we are, naked, we start running through the house. Without making a sound we move through the rooms in the dark, along the hall, up and down the stairs. We stand still outside my parents' bedroom and then go on, out of the front door and into the garden, naked despite the cold, onto the lawn and then back downstairs again to my room.

Suddenly my dad's standing in the room in pyjama trousers and a top.

'Out, get out now – ' and he grabs hold of Andi and drags him, past my mother who's screaming, up the stairs and throws him out of the house.

I run back down the stairs, lock my door from the inside and climb out of the window with our things. My dad shouts after us.

On the way to his parents' Andi gets the pen out. We put our tag everywhere, on every wall, every drive, every garage door, his name and my name together. Andi and Tina together. The pen passes from him to me and back again. No and, no hearts, just our tag – exactly as we are, side by side, on everything all the way to his.

And then when we're outside the door he says: well then –

Brief pause.

I love you but we'll never see each other again. Yes, I say, I know. Take care. Goodbye.

11

Two days earlier. The apartment is already being packed up. The parents are packing. The son carries a box out of his room and puts it in the hallway. Nobody takes any notice of it. He stands there for a moment.

Then he goes over to the wall and draws a sign on it with a thick black pen: a coded name; a tag.

FRANK: Stop it –

ANDI: Why –

FRANK: You don't do that –

ANDI: Why not –

FRANK: You're going to ruin the walls –

ANDI: The walls –

FRANK: Yes, the walls –

ANDI: The walls are already ruined –

Brief pause.

In a couple of days the decorators are going to come and paint everything after nineteen years –

FRANK: Ruined? These walls aren't ruined. They've had wear and tear, maybe, but they're not ruined – ruining them's what you're doing – nobody's going to be able to paint over that mark –

ANDI: So much the better –

FRANK has a small pot of paint and paints over the mark with a roller. The paint is special paint which doesn't cover the mark.

FRANK: Look, it won't go away,

He paints over the mark again –

it keeps coming through – look at it –

12.1

Two days later, shortly after half past three in the morning.

ROMY: (*Feeling her head bandage which is slowly leaking blood.*) What happened to my head? Do you know?

ANDI: No –

ROMY: You don't?

ANDI: You're hurt.

ROMY: Yes – and I don't know what did it. I must have been hit by something.

Brief pause.

When I woke up I was back here.

ANDI shrugs his shoulders.

I was out – I don't know what happened before.

So how did you know I was here?

No answer.

You knew that – I'd be here when you came back. Didn't you?

No answer. ANDI carries on putting his things into the box which toppled over. While he's doing it he looks at individual pieces of his childhood. Cars, Indians, lego.

Silence. He's got a matchbox car in his hand.

ANDI: This old racing-car, it's got wings –

He demonstrates the way the car can spread its wings.

Its doors are like wings.

Then he throws the car into the box.

ROMY:

'Who knows how long I've loved you
You know I love you still
Will I wait a lonely lifetime
If you want me to – I will'

D'you know that?

ANDI: The song? Sure –

Brief pause.

ROMY: You know it?

ANDI: Sure I know it.

Brief pause.

But where do you know it from?

He throws the last of the things into the box. He has now cleared everything away. He closes the box, which is not especially full, and marks it with a large example of his tag.

See?

ROMY: What?

ANDI: This tag – before it was just some box. And now – now it's mine. That's what the tag's for. That box belongs to me. I've just got the one – I don't need more than one box.

12.2

Later that night.

ANDI: It was a stone.

ROMY: What was a stone –

ANDI: It was a stone that hit you.

ROMY: No –

ANDI: Yes – it was a stone – 'bout this big – it hit you on the head there.

ROMY: How do you know that?

12.3

A little earlier the same night. He closes the box, which isn't especially full, and marks it with a large version of his symbol.

ANDI: See?

ROMY: What?

ANDI: This tag – before it was just some box. And now – now it's mine. That's what the tag's for. That box belongs to me. I've just got the one – I don't need more than one box.

Brief pause.

ROMY: Have you got a girlfriend?

ANDI: Yeah.

ROMY: What's her name?

ANDI: Tina.

ROMY: Where is she now?

ANDI: At home. Or on the way there.

ROMY: Why isn't she here.

Brief pause.

ANDI: No room.

ROMY: I see –

Brief pause.

Why aren't you at her place –

ANDI: I was – till just now.

ROMY: Do you love her?

ANDI: A lot.

ROMY: How much do you love her?

ANDI: I'll love her for ever.

ROMY: For ever?

ANDI: For ever –

ROMY: Does she know that?

ANDI: She knows.

. ı : Did you tell her that?

ANDI: I told her.

ROMY: You did?

ANDI: Yeah, I said – I'd always love her.

Brief pause.

ROMY: What does she look like?

ANDI: I'd paint her if I could – but I can't.

Brief pause.

I'd fill up a whole building with her, her body stretched across a massive wall. What I'd paint on the wall would be a forest, a forest that her body would be made of, branches, twigs, leaves, all living, indestructible, growing while you watched, her body would be there on the wall in blue leaves, supple, evolving. A wall, a forest, a body – dark, gleaming. That's how I'd have to paint her, mysterious, dazzling –

There are animals, voices. An amazing bright green when I wake up next to her. Behind it black. Tigers. Parrots. A place that cannot exist. Confusion, beauty, darkness, that's also her body. A darkness you'll never be able to live inside. A few rays of sunlight fall on a lake. There are people swimming, a couple. That's what you'd have to paint on the wall, the roots and the fishes. That's my girlfriend's body, her youth and everything that's still to come: other men, another life. Children.

The way she moves.

A wall-painting that's nothing but forest, a wall full of forest, nothing else, except for where someone has put tiny windows high up into the wall.

Brief pause.

ROMY: And her face?

ANDI: Her face –

Brief pause.

ROMY: Her face –

ANDI: Her face is the sky. The sky above the building, above the wall. The chimneys are her neck. The clouds are her hair and the sky, that you can see right through but never reach the end, her eyes.

Brief pause.

ROMY: Incredible, you're so like your father. When he was young.

Brief pause.

ANDI: It was a stone.

ROMY: What kind of stone –

ANDI: It was a stone that hit you.

ROMY: No –

ANDI: Yes – it was a stone – 'bout this big – it hit you on the head there.

ROMY: How do you know that?

ANDI: I know because I threw it.

ROMY: You –

ANDI: Yeah, me. I did it.

ROMY: Then you were the one who brought me back here –

ANDI: I was, yeah –

ROMY: You brought me here – not your father.

ANDI: No, I – I thought you were dead –

ROMY goes up to the young man and kisses him passionately.

12.4

Shortly beforehand.

TINA: He said we'd never see each other again. He said he loved me but we'd never see each other again.

Brief pause.

And then he vanishes inside the building. And I – I think he's going to come straight back out again. He did say we'd never see each other again, but what's he going to do there, in that flat. Where there's no room for him. He's put the light on inside – but I can't see any more than that.

I stand there outside, waiting for him to come back, it's cold.

Brief pause.

I wait five minutes, ten, but he doesn't come.

I stand alone in the dark at the bottom of the bank, just beyond the light from the street-lamps. Everything's sleeping. No cars. No voices.

Above me high in the air an aeroplane. What's it like up there, right now, in that plane?

Nobody on the streets. I carry on waiting. And he doesn't come back.

12.5

A little later. The son and the woman in the hallway. She has had sex with him.

ROMY: What about your girlfriend now –

ANDI: What about her?

ROMY: You're going to love her for ever – isn't that what you promised –

ANDI: (*Laughs.*) I said that, yeah –

Brief pause.

ROMY: So?

ANDI: It doesn't matter –

ROMY: Why not?

ANDI: Because I'm never going to see her again.

ROMY: Aren't you?

ANDI: No, I'm never going to see her again.

ROMY: How do you know –

ANDI: I know.

ROMY: You could stay here.

Brief pause.

Or come back.

ANDI: No.

ROMY: Why not?

ANDI: Because it's over. Simple as that.

Now he bends down and kisses her. During the kiss she reaches out for a plastic bag which had previously appeared during the search for bandages and finds the one with the Eiffel Tower on it.

They disappear into his room.

12.6

Around ten hours earlier.

CLAUDIA: Look –

She holds the bag up.

Take a good look at this bag.

He needs a moment before he thinks of looking at the writing on the bag. The bag has a picture of the Eiffel Tower.

FRANK: No!

CLAUDIA: See where this is from?

FRANK: You've –

Brief pause.

You've kept it all this time – you're not telling me you've kept that for nineteen years.

12.7

Approximately ten hours later.

The son and the woman. Shortly after they disappeared into his room, they come back out again. They kiss, he laughs and continues trying to kiss her while she, continuing to kiss him, tries to pull the plastic bag over his head.

They disappear back into his room.

They appear again, this time she has already pulled the bag over his eyes. While they are kissing he tries to half-free himself, even though he's not yet willing to understand what is happening.

They disappear back inside his room.

When they re-enter he tries to escape but can't, she's pulled the bag over his head. He grabs at thin air. He can't breathe. He is going to die.

Back into his room. He struggles his way, blind and suffocating, back into the hallway, she pulls him back into his room.

Through another door, the mother enters, wearing knickers and a baggy t-shirt. She's extremely sleepy. Did she hear something?

CLAUDIA: Andi?

Nothing. She goes into the bathroom and shuts the door behind her. Noises from the bathroom.

The son, by now fighting for his life, has made it back into the hallway, we hear the sound of the toilet flushing, but ROMY VOGTLÄNDER pulls him back into his room.

The mother comes back out of the bathroom and goes back into her room.

The son crawls out of his room one last time.

ROMY VOGTLÄNDER pulls him back.

13

The following morning. FRANK and CLAUDIA in the hallway. ANDI's tag on the wall.

FRANK: You're old.

Pause.

You look old.

Pause.

CLAUDIA: So do you.

FRANK: Old and clapped out.

CLAUDIA: (*Quietly.*) Like you.

Brief pause.

Though unlike you I'm not a coward with it.

FRANK: You're old, clapped out and ugly.

Brief pause.

He does something to one of the boxes.

Not much left now.

Brief pause.

CLAUDIA: What you just said –

Brief pause.

You don't say that to anyone – what you just said – not even after nineteen years of marriage.

Brief pause.

You just don't say that.

Not after I raised your son. And definitely not when you're planning a future together – like we are –

Brief pause.

You just don't say that.

14

A few minutes earlier on the same morning. FRANK is in the hallway, CLAUDIA enters.

FRANK: Sleep well?

CLAUDIA: Bad dreams. Been having bad dreams half the night.

She opens the door to the son's room.

FRANK: She's gone. No one there.

CLAUDIA: Where's Andi?

FRANK: Andi? He's not there – his room's empty.

CLAUDIA: Where is he?

FRANK: How should I know – bound to be at Tina's.

CLAUDIA: Hardly – her father hates him.

FRANK: He must have stayed somewhere.

Pause.

CLAUDIA: That's a pity.

FRANK: Hm?

CLAUDIA: I said, that's a pity.

FRANK: What do you mean –

CLAUDIA: That she's gone – you must think that's a pity.

FRANK: Why d'you say that?

CLAUDIA: Because it's true –

FRANK: What –

CLAUDIA: It must be a pity for you that she's gone.

FRANK: Why should it be – what gives you the idea that I might possibly regret –

CLAUDIA: Because you'd have liked to have another conversation with her.

FRANK: Yeah?

CLAUDIA: Yeah –

FRANK: What about?

CLAUDIA: What about?

FRANK: Yeah, what about? What would I have wanted to have a conversation with her about –

CLAUDIA: I dunno – you ought to know that better than me –

FRANK: I don't understand what you're talking about.

Brief pause.

If I'd wanted to have a conversation with her then I could simply have asked her to come in. Yesterday. Instead of throwing her out.

CLAUDIA: Oh right –

FRANK: Yeah –

CLAUDIA: But you didn't throw her out.

Brief pause.

I was the one who shut the door, not you.

Brief pause.

You put her to bed. You bandaged her head.

FRANK: What was I supposed to do –

CLAUDIA: Nothing –

FRANK: Nothing –

CLAUDIA: But instead you keep going back into the room to check how she is – though she wasn't even conscious!

FRANK: That's why. She was badly hurt. I was afraid she'd never wake up again.

CLAUDIA: This fear – which is only coming out now – was totally unfounded. This fear was just a pretext. A pretext to look at that woman.

Pause.

And it was our last evening here.

FRANK: You're old.

Pause.

You look old.

Pause.

CLAUDIA: So do you.

FRANK: Old and clapped out.

CLAUDIA: (*Quietly.*) Like you.

Brief pause.

Though unlike you I'm not a coward with it.

FRANK: You're old, clapped out and ugly.

Brief pause.

He does something to one of the boxes.

Not much left now.

Brief pause.

CLAUDIA: What you just said –

Brief pause.

You don't say that to anyone – what you said – not even after nineteen years of marriage.

Brief pause.

You just don't say that.

Not after I raised your son. And definitely not when you're planning a future together – like we are –

Brief pause.

You just don't say that.

Enter ROMY VOGTLÄNDER. She uses the open front door.

ROMY: This door's had it – the lock's practically fallen out. How on earth did that happen? What was it?

Brief pause.

It's beyond repair.

Silence.

I'm back. Hello.

Silence.

CLAUDIA: I'm going to leave this flat now. In twenty minutes –

She looks at her watch.

In twenty minutes I'm going to come back and if this woman's still here, I'm going to leave for ever. If this woman is still here in twenty minutes, then everything there ever was between us will be over.

CLAUDIA exits. She slams the front door, which of course swings back open again.

15

Approximately twenty-five minutes later.

CLAUDIA enters the flat. The hallway is deserted. Noises from the bathroom. She stands outside and listens. Goes into the neighbouring rooms, looking around. Nobody there. She comes back, stops by the bathroom door, still listening.

CLAUDIA: Well –

Brief pause.

Well, she's gone!

Brief pause. She's pleased.

I almost didn't think you could do it.

Almost.

She turns back to the open front door and tries again to close it. Her attempts become increasingly violent and eventually she kicks the door shut so hard that it does indeed stay shut.

I've fixed the door.

(*Quietly.*) The fucking cunt.

(*At the bathroom door.*) Can I come in?

The door is locked.

I almost didn't think you could do it.

Brief pause.

Are you having a shower?

(*Slightly hubristic.*) Nineteen years of marriage stick. They just won't go away – no – they stick a lot longer than one summer.

Brief pause.

Was that Tina, who just came out of the building? I thought I saw someone –

She finds a small wrapped present. Talks in the direction of the bathroom –

What's this? Is this from Tina? That's nice of her. That's really nice of her – how charming. D'you know what's inside?

Brief pause.

What about Andi? Is Andi not here? Where is he? Is one box all he's got?

She is almost about to open that one box and look at what's inside but then she pauses.

She takes the present and goes into her room. On the way into the room she tears off the wrapping-paper. She stands in the doorway for a moment, puzzled.

16.1

Approximately twenty-five minutes earlier. The front door bangs shut and swings open again. CLAUDIA has left the flat. FRANK and ROMY VOGTLÄNDER are alone.

Brief pause.

FRANK: And now?

Brief pause.

ROMY: Now all we have to do is wait for her to come back.

Then we'll be alone at last.

FRANK: No!

ROMY: Whatever – we can go before she comes back –

Brief pause.

Okay – come on then –

She goes to the door. He stands still.

FRANK: No –

ROMY: What do you mean no –

Brief pause.

FRANK: I don't want you to be here when she comes back.

Brief pause.

ROMY: You want me to leave?

FRANK: Yes.

Brief pause.

I want you to leave. The sooner the better.

Brief pause.

ROMY: I've got a present for her –

FRANK: For who –

ROMY: For your wife –

FRANK: She won't open it.

ROMY: Who knows –

FRANK: Right –

Brief pause.

Take your present and get out –

ROMY: I don't believe you.

FRANK: What –

ROMY: That you want me to leave. That you want to stay. I don't believe you.

Brief pause.

You're not going to send me away. You carried me into the room. You bandaged my head.

FRANK: Last night, yes – you were hurt. You needed help.

Brief pause.

But now – you're better now.

Brief pause.

And all of a sudden you're back. Why? What do you want?

ROMY: I want to be with you, what else –

FRANK: But you can see how it is.

ROMY: I can see that, yes.

FRANK: So –

Brief pause.

ROMY: You love me.

FRANK: What gives you that idea?

ROMY: It's true.

And your wife's just left the flat. She's finally left us alone. She's going to come back in twenty minutes. And then she'll be gone for ever.

Brief pause.

That's what's going to happen.

FRANK: That's not going to happen.

ROMY: Why not –

FRANK: Because we've been married for nineteen years.

16.2

A couple of minutes later.

FRANK: Okay then – let's go.

He looks for his jacket.

Let's go. You're right.

Brief pause.

There's not much here any more – not much left.

ROMY: Your wife –

FRANK: My wife's gone and she'll see that it's over. Simple as that.

Brief pause.

ROMY: What about your son –

It's not enough, just giving up your wife. You've got to give up your son too.

16.3

A few minutes earlier.

FRANK: What gives you that idea?

ROMY: It's true.

And your wife's just left the flat. She's finally left us alone. She's going to come back in twenty minutes. And then she'll be gone for ever.

Brief pause.

That's what's going to happen.

FRANK: That's not going to happen.

ROMY: Why not –

FRANK: Because we've been married for nineteen years.

ROMY: These nineteen years of marriage – I can't see them.

FRANK: Right now those nineteen years take up more than an entire container!

Brief pause.

Seventy packing-cases!

ROMY: And where is this container?

FRANK: Gone! The rest will follow –

ROMY: Right –

Brief pause.

What do you think? What do you imagine I've been doing all this time? For the last twenty-four years? What was there? Men – not one, lots of them, one after another, think of a job, actors, doctors, lawyers, artists, what do you want to know about? Their homes, their cars? The holidays? Or the split-ups? What do you think I've been doing for the last twenty-four years? I was rarely alone, but I've always been waiting – because none of them, not one, was like you were then, none of them could be anything more than what they were supposed to be – there was nothing there, no freedom, nothing, all those years everything as planned. Pre-programmed. Sketches. Don't tell me now – don't go telling me that you're exactly the same.

Brief pause.

FRANK: Okay then – let's go.

He looks for his jacket.

Let's go. You're right.

Brief pause.

There's not much here any more – not much left.

ROMY: Your wife –

FRANK: My wife's gone and she'll see that it's over. Simple as that.

Brief pause.

ROMY: What about your son –

It's not enough, just giving up your wife. You've got to give up your son too.

Brief pause. He doesn't understand.

FRANK: How am I supposed to give up my son?

She shrugs her shoulders.

I mean: even if I leave here, he's still going to be my son.

He'll still exist, – just like the last twenty-four years will still exist – the whole time without you.

ROMY: I insist, I need to hear you say it –

Brief pause.

otherwise we won't be happy –

FRANK: What? What do you need to hear? You wanted me to come with you, I'm willing to do that, what more do you want?

ROMY: You've got to say it,

Brief pause.

You've got to say it out loud – that all those years never happened.

FRANK: No.

ROMY: No?

Brief pause.

In that case I'll go now –

She goes to the door.

FRANK: They did exist, they happened, here – what can I say –

ROMY: Then at least say it would have been better if they hadn't existed: your wife, your marriage and your son.

FRANK: That's not going to happen.

ROMY: It's got to.

FRANK: Why –

ROMY: There's no other way.

Pause. Nothing. She turns to face the door, takes hold of the handle, exits –

FRANK: Yes! It's possible –

It is possible that –

She comes back.

ROMY: What –

FRANK: That it would have been better,

ROMY: What –

FRANK: That it would have been better not to have had a wife and a son: it's possible, yes, it is possible – come back –

She comes back and kisses him. They kiss for a long time.

ROMY: Now sing –

Sing me the song.

Pause.

FRANK: I can't –

Brief pause.

Laughs.

I've forgotten the words, I've even forgotten the tune –

ROMY: You've forgotten the song?

FRANK: No – I – I just can't remember how it goes –

ROMY VOGTLÄNDER sings 'I Will' by Lennon / McCartney.

ROMY: Now do you remember?

FRANK: Yes –

ROMY: What else do you remember?

FRANK: Everything –

ROMY: What –

FRANK: You – us –

ROMY: What –

FRANK: Your room. The school. Your parents.

Brief pause.

ROMY: What was the name of the park – do you remember the park?

FRANK: The park – I don't know – did it have a name?

ROMY: But you remember the sunrise in the park –

Brief pause.

FRANK: The sun was still low down behind the hills in the east, it slowly got lighter and one by one the birds started singing in the dark trees. The edge of the forest behind us. A wall of forest. Nobody else there. Just us. Hadn't slept. In love. We went there a lot that summer. And we never felt cold.

ROMY: I mean the sunrise when I gave you the present –

FRANK: The present –

He has no idea what she's talking about.

ROMY: The present – don't you remember the present?

FRANK: Ye-es –

Brief pause.

ROMY: No you don't. You haven't got a clue what I'm talking about.

Brief pause.

You don't remember the present.

Brief pause.

FRANK: This present – what present – it's so long ago!

Brief pause.

I can't just miss out all the time in between.

ROMY: In other words, you're not coming.

Brief pause.

You said you were going to come with me.

Brief pause.

But you can't.

Brief pause.

You can't even remember!

FRANK: What – what can I say – I don't know what your present was.

ROMY: Then I'm going to leave here all by myself and you're going to stay here all by yourself with nothing.

ROMY VOGTLÄNDER leaves the apartment.

17

The husband alone in the hallway. He doesn't move. Then he unbuttons his shirt, ready to go into the bathroom. Someone knocks on the front door, which is only leaning shut anyway.

Nothing. More knocking. Nothing.

TINA: Hello?

No answer. FRANK stands in the hallway as if paralysed.

Hello?

Pause.

FRANK: The door's open.

TINA enters the apartment, shy and hesitant. TINA and FRANK stand facing each other.

FRANK: Tina –

Brief pause.

TINA is surprised that no one else seems to be there.

TINA: I want to talk to Andi.

FRANK: Andi?

Brief pause.

He's not here.

TINA: He – he's not here?

FRANK: No – he's not – I thought he was with you?

TINA: No, he isn't –

Brief pause.

He's got to be here –

FRANK: But I'm telling you: he's not here –

TINA: He's got to be here – he can't be anywhere else –

FRANK: What makes you think that –

TINA: I saw him come into the building –

FRANK: When?

TINA: Last night –

FRANK: He wasn't here last night –

TINA: Yes he was – I saw him myself – and anyway:

Brief pause.

That's his tag! He was here.

FRANK: Okay –

Brief pause.

Maybe he was here for a while – and then he went out again.

TINA: He didn't.

FRANK: Why not?

TINA: Because I was waiting for him outside the building.

FRANK: Since when?

TINA: Since last night, 'bout half past three.

He looks at her sceptically.

FRANK: Since half past three in the morning?

TINA: Yeah – since he came in here.

FRANK: You've been waiting outside the building since half past three in the morning?

TINA: (*In tears.*) Yes – but he didn't come out again.

Pause.

FRANK: His room's empty. I'm sorry. He's not here.

TINA looks into the empty room.

TINA runs away crying.

TINA: He must be, he's got to be here.

FRANK is left standing in the hallway. Then he gets hold of the roller which is on top of the pot with the paint inside, but he has second thoughts: he doesn't paint over the tag again. He puts the roller back down again. He takes his shirt off. He goes into the bathroom and locks the door behind him.

18

CLAUDIA enters the flat. The hallway is deserted. Noises from the bathroom. She stands outside and listens. Goes into the neighbouring rooms, looking around. Nobody there. She comes back, stops by the bathroom door, still listening.

CLAUDIA: Well –

Brief pause.

Well, she's gone!

Brief pause. She's pleased.

I almost didn't think you could do it.

Almost.

She turns back to the open front door and tries again to close it. Her attempts become increasingly violent and eventually she kicks the door shut so hard that it does indeed stay shut.

I've fixed the door.

(*Quietly.*) The fucking cunt.

(*At the bathroom door.*) Can I come in?

The door is locked.

I almost didn't think you could do it.

Brief pause.

Are you having a shower?

Slightly hubristic.

Nineteen years of marriage stick. They just won't go away – no – they stick a lot longer than one summer.

Brief pause.

Was that Tina, who just came out of the building? I thought I saw someone –

She finds a small wrapped present. Talks in the direction of the bathroom –

What's this? Is this from Tina? That's nice of her. That's really nice of her – how charming. D'you know what's inside?

Brief pause.

What about Andi? Is Andi not here? Where is he? Is one box all he's got?

She is almost about to open that one box and look at what's inside but then she pauses.

She takes the present and goes into her room. On the way into the room she tears off the wrapping-paper. She stands in the doorway for a moment, puzzled and looks at the present – apparently nothing more than a plastic bag with the Eiffel Tower on it – a look back to the bathroom. She exits into her room. Shortly after she has gone: a piercing scream.

19

TINA: I can't leave – I can't leave there, I can't.

Brief pause.

I can't leave the place where Andi must be and isn't. Where can he have gone? He has to be there but he isn't there. I run back and forth in panic, I wait at the top of the bank where we always used to meet, where we –

Brief pause.

Where we threw the stones, I sit there, alone, I even throw stones, at nothing, because no one comes in and no one goes out, except for Andi's mother who goes into the building and then I walk around again, back and forth, up and down, eventually I go all the way round the building, from the back, behind the building, you can see into Andi's parents' bedroom, with the fitted wardrobes and the big bed and suddenly Claudia, Andi's mother, staggers into the room, she's surprised or maybe even confused, she's got a plastic bag in her hands, I get the feeling I've seen that bag before.

Brief pause.

She's still standing in the doorway, undecided, uncertain, only then does she go into the room, holding the bag, there's something she doesn't understand, that much I can see. She reaches inside the bag, it seems to be empty from out here, at least that's what it looks like through the window and the moment, the moment she reaches inside the bag, at least that's what it looks like through the window, her fingers, her hands, her arms suddenly catch fire. There in her bedroom the woman catches fire all over, she's burning, her whole body is burning, she burns so quickly so horribly – she doesn't even seem to be able to scream – I scream, I scream as loud as I can but who's going to hear me – and then Andi's father appears in the doorway, he sees his wife on fire with the molten remains of the bag in her hand and he stands there not moving until he vanishes from the doorway again. I run. The removal van's coming down the street and stops in front of the building. Where's Andi –

20

A moment earlier. FRANK comes out of the shower, he's got a towel wrapped round his hips. Apart from that, he's naked and rather wet.

He walks into the hallway and falls clumsily when he treads on a matchbox car. The car skids away under his foot. FRANK stands up and treads very painfully on a plastic Indian. Then he looks down at the floor. He slowly discovers a scattering of tiny bits of toys: most of them are to be found behind ANDI's box. He gathers up everything he can find and is about to put it in ANDI's box. FRANK opens the box (and discovers his son's dead body). Speechless shock. He drops everything he has just gathered up. He tries to get to his wife in the bedroom, falls over another matchbox car, possibly one that he just dropped in shock. He gets up, falls over again, maybe he has now injured his cruciate ligament or something similar.

He hops and crawls to the bedroom, opens the door and stops motionless in the doorway for a moment – he sees his wife on fire – where now?

In sheer panic he tries to get to the front door. Somehow he manages to walk, hop, fall, crawl his way there. He tries the door handle.

The door does not open. He doesn't understand. He tries the handle again. The door is wedged so tightly shut that it won't open again. There's a ring at the door. He can't even get up. Both his knees are useless. There's another ring. He can't open the door and can't get to the intercom.

The End.